Berkshire

A concise and Detailed Itinerary Handbook to a
Memorable Adventure, Discovery and Insider's
Experiences

BONUS:

- Itinerary
- Useful Phrases
- Family Vacation
- Solo Traveler
- Romantic Adventures
- Delectable Images

BERKSHIRE
Travel Guide
2023

Elis Tello Rios

*A concise and Detailed Itinerary
Handbook to a Memorable Adventure,
Discovery and Insider's Experiences*

Elis Tello Rios

Table of Contents

INTRODUCTION

Welcome to Berkshire

Welcome to Berkshire, an area that perfectly captures the spirit of traditional English charm. The southern English county of Berkshire is a veritable treasure mine of natural splendor, extensive history, and cultural experiences.

Every tourist may find something to enjoy in Berkshire, whether they're looking for a tranquil rural hideaway, to explore historical sites, or to indulge in delicious cuisine.

As soon as I set foot in the gorgeous region of Berkshire, I was immediately surrounded by enthralling sights and sensations. This area, tucked away among undulating hills and lush meadows, begs to be explored. Before me, a tapestry of human culture, natural beauty, and history emerged, promising an extraordinary journey.

I stood at the brink of Windsor Castle admiring its majesty as the sun's soft rays bathed the sky with gold colors. The walls muttered legends of kings and timeless events. As I traveled through the beautiful towns and villages, I had a feeling of belonging as residents joyfully embraced their culture and shared tales that had been handed down through the decades.

I found secret treasures tucked away in nature's embrace as I wandered the lovely trees and winding pathways. Wildflower scents swirled in the air, and singing bird sounds joined me as I traveled. I strolled down the Thames River, seeing life's ups and downs in its placid waters.

Each destination revealed a different aspect of Berkshire's attractiveness, from the vivid colors of Ascot Racecourse to the tranquil serenity of The Savill Garden. I indulged in gastronomic treats, tasting regional foods in lively markets and savoring traditional treats that tantalized my taste buds with each mouthful.

However, Berkshire's residents were the ones who gave this tour its unique character. Every connection was infused with their warmth and kindness, turning strangers into friends. Their affection for their country inspired me to fall in love with this captivating place as well.

I came to see that Berkshire was more than just a location on a map; it was a tapestry of experiences woven with threads of beauty and awe as the sun sunk below the horizon, sending a golden light over the countryside. Thus, I set out on my journey, anxious to share Berkshire's beauty and reveal its secrets while also encouraging other travelers to forge their own priceless experiences there.

With its undulating hills, stunning scenery, and quaint villages, Berkshire encourages you to set off on a life-changing journey of exploration and first-hand encounters. In this enchanted region of England, immerse yourself in the rich local culture, discover off-the-beaten-path hidden jewels, and make lifelong memories.

1.2 About This Travel Guide

Your invaluable travel companion for exploring Berkshire's top attractions is this travel guide. It is intended to serve as a brief but comprehensive itinerary manual and provides insightful information, useful advice, and insider suggestions to help you have an amazing and flawless experience.

You may discover in-depth details on the biggest tourist destinations, outdoor activities, cultural experiences, and secret spots in Berkshire within these pages. Explore world-famous sites like Windsor Castle and Ascot Racecourse, explore the area's natural beauties, immerse yourself in the local arts and music scene, and enjoy the culinary options to experience the tastes of Berkshire.

This book also offers helpful planning advice, such as the ideal time to visit, travel choices, suggested lodgings, and helpful hints for a hassle-free and pleasurable vacation.

This guide will serve as your go-to resource, helping you discover Berkshire's mysteries and making sure your trip is nothing short of amazing whether you're a frequent traveler or a first-time visitor. Prepare to go on a voyage of a lifetime as you explore Berkshire's enchantment, beauty, and undiscovered gems.

Chapter 2: Getting to Know Berkshire

2.1 About Berkshire

The county of Berkshire, which is located in southern England, is renowned for its gorgeous scenery, ancient sites, and thriving cultural life. The county is close to important cities like London and Oxford thanks to its borders with Oxfordshire, Buckinghamshire, Surrey, and Hampshire.

Approximately 1,262 square kilometers in size, Berkshire is home to attractive cities, lovely villages, and vast rural areas. Visitors may enjoy a beautiful fusion of rustic charm and natural beauty thanks to the region's diversified landscape, which includes rolling hills, lush meadows, and the picturesque River Thames.

2.2 History and Culture

Berkshire is proud of its extensive, centuries-old historical legacy. Since Windsor Castle, the official house of the British monarchy, was built there, it has been linked to the history of the royal family. Other historical monuments in the county, like the remains of Reading Abbey, Highclere Castle (better known as Downton Abbey), and Basildon Park, provide a window into the history of the area.

In Berkshire, there is a thriving and diversified cultural environment. The county holds a lot of festivals, musical events, and theater productions all year round. Every art aficionado may find something to appreciate, from historical folk festivals to modern art exhibits.

The cultural history and creative accomplishments of the county are shown through museums and art galleries including The River & Rowing Museum and Reading Museum.

2.3 Geography and Climate

The topography of Berkshire is characterized by rolling hills, woods, and wide-open spaces. The western portion of the county is bordered by the North Wessex Downs, an Area of Outstanding Natural Beauty, which offers possibilities for outdoor recreation and picturesque hikes.

In general, Berkshire has moderate winters and pleasant summers. Between 20 and 25 degrees

Celsius (68 to 77 degrees Fahrenheit) are the typical summer temperatures, whereas 36 to 46 degrees Fahrenheit are the typical winter temperatures.

Because it rains every day of the year, it's a good idea to bring an umbrella or a lightweight waterproof jacket.

2.4 Local Etiquettes and Customs

Visitors should be aware of the regional traditions and etiquette in Berkshire as well as most of England. Here are some crucial points:

a) In Berkshire, kindness and politeness are highly regarded. It is usual to use the words "please" and "thank you" in social situations.

b) In public venues like stores or attractions, people are expected to patiently wait in line. Queuing is a significant part of British society.

c) It's crucial to respect others' personal space. Unless essential, keep your distance from other people, and always get permission before taking a picture of someone.

d) If the service fee is not already included in the bill, it is typical to tip between 10% and 15% of the entire price while eating out.

e) It is advised to be on time for appointments or other planned events since punctuality is valued.

You may make sure that your trip to Berkshire is polite and pleasurable by being acquainted with the regional traditions and manners.

Chapter 3: Getting Started with Your Travel Plans

3. The Ideal Season to Visit Berkshire

Your interests and the activities you want to do will determine when is the ideal time to visit Berkshire. The county has a pleasant temperature all year round, making it a popular vacation spot. The seasons are broken out as follows:

Spring (March to May): Spring is the best season for outdoor activities and touring gardens like The Savill Garden since it delivers blossoming flowers and comfortable weather. However, bear in mind that rainfall is typical for this time of year.

Summer (June to August): Berkshire is more well-liked throughout the summer because of the pleasant, sunny weather. It's ideal for visiting events like Royal Ascot, taking in outdoor festivals, and seeing the countryside. But it may become congested, particularly in popular tourist destinations.

Autumn (September to November): As the leaves change colors, Berkshire experiences stunning greenery throughout the autumn season. It's a fantastic time to take strolls and explore historical locations like Windsor Castle. Although it is a pleasant day, there may be some rain.

Winter (December to February): Berkshire's winters might be cold, but they also have a certain allure. Holiday markets, ice skating rinks, and a warm atmosphere all come with the season. Additionally, it's a great time to explore indoor attractions like art galleries and museums.

3.2 Duration of Stay

Your schedule and the pursuit of the activities you want to engage in will determine how long you will be in Berkshire. It is advised to stay for at least 2-3 days to thoroughly see the county's attractions. This amount of time permits seeing significant sites like Windsor Castle, touring the countryside, and taking in the local culture. However, you may wish to prolong your stay to a week or more if you have particular hobbies or want to partake in a lot of outdoor activities.

3.3 Visas and Travel Documents

You could require a visa to enter the country if you're a citizen of a nation other than the UK or the EU. It's crucial to research the necessary visas well in advance of your trip. For the most recent information on visa requirements, go to the UK government's official website or get in touch with the British embassy or consulate in your area.

A valid passport should be carried together with any other essential travel papers, including travel insurance, airline tickets, hotel reservations, and evidence of enough money to pay your expenditures while you are away.

3.3 Transportation Alternatives

Berkshire has excellent transit connections and a range of choices for getting around:

a) By Air: London Heathrow Airport (LHR) and London Gatwick Airport (LGW) are the closest international airports to Berkshire. From there, taking a rail, bus, or cab will put you right in Berkshire.

b) By Train: There are good train links across the county, with regular services to and from London and other significant cities. Berkshire's primary train stations are Reading Windsor & Eton Central, and Maidenhead.

c) By Car: Berkshire is readily accessible by car because of the region's extensive network of main roads. The county is conveniently accessible from London and other areas of England because of the M4 highway, which passes through it. In big cities and airports, you may rent a vehicle.

d) By Public Transportation: Berkshire has a dependable public transportation network that includes buses and local trains and offers easy access to the county's many towns, tourist destinations, and rural regions.

3.5 Accommodation Options

Berkshire has a variety of lodging choices to fit every need and desire. The county is home to upscale hotels, inviting bed & breakfasts, self-catering cottages, and quaint inns.

There are many hotels and guesthouses in well-known cities like Windsor, Reading, and Newbury, while the countryside has charming farm stays and rural getaways. It is advised to reserve your lodging in advance, particularly during the busiest travel times, to ensure that you get your first option.

Berkshire lodging may be found and compared via online travel directories, hotel booking services, and government tourist websites. To choose the choice that best satisfies your demands and budget, take into account variables like location, facilities, and reviews.

Chapter 4: 10 Top Attractions in Berkshire

4.1 Windsor Castle

One of Berkshire's most well-known landmarks is Windsor Castle, which is situated in the town of Windsor. The official seat of the British monarchy, it is the biggest and oldest inhabited castle in the world. What you need to know is as follows:

a) Learn more about the State Apartments: The State Apartments are exquisitely furnished and include stunning artwork, historical relics, and opulent furniture. The lavish St. George's Hall and the magnificent Queen Mary's Dolls' House are not to be missed.

b) Visit St. George's Chapel: King Henry VIII and Queen Elizabeth the Queen Mother are among the British monarchs who were laid to rest at this magnificent specimen of Gothic architecture. Attend the lovely choral services or perhaps take in the exquisite workmanship.

c) Witness the Changing of the Guard: On certain days, the Changing of the Guard ritual is performed with pomp and spectacle. To properly organize your visit, check the schedule in advance.

d) Take a trip around the expansive grounds of the castle, which include the lovely gardens and the peaceful Long Walk, which provides sweeping views of the surrounding countryside.

4.2 Ascot Racecourse

A must-see destination for racing aficionados is Ascot Racecourse, which is located in the town of Ascot and is known for hosting important horse racing events. Here's what to anticipate:

a) Attend Royal Ascot: In June, the renowned horse racing festival Royal Ascot draws spectators from all around the globe. Don your best dress, and take in the exciting races, and the gorgeous setting.

b) Discover the Racecourse: Ascot Racecourse has several race meets throughout the year, including outside of Royal Ascot. Place your bets while taking part in the thrill of horse racing and supporting your favorite horse.

c) Visit the Parade Ring and Paddock: Go to the Parade Ring and Paddock area to get up close to the racehorses and jockeys. It's a great chance to see the horses' preparations and see them before the races.

d) Take Advantage of the Facilities: Ascot Racecourse has several eating establishments, pubs, and hospitality suites where you may unwind and take in the energetic environment. Enjoy fine dining while toasting the excitement of horse racing.

4.3 The Savill Garden

The Savill Garden, a horticultural treasure in Windsor Great Park, is home to an outstanding assortment of plants and breathtaking scenery. What makes it unique is as follows:

a) Learn More About the Gardens: The Savill Garden offers a wide variety of themed gardens, such as the Hidden Gardens, the Summer

Gardens, and the New Zealand Garden. Each location has its charm and a profusion of vibrant flowers.

b) Discover the Savill Building: This architectural wonder is home to a restaurant, a store, and a visitor center. Take in the panoramic views while dining, look around for one-of-a-kind presents, or ask the helpful staff for guidance.

c) Take a Guided Tour: Sign up for a tour that is given by knowledgeable gardeners who will provide intriguing details about the plant collections, horticultural practices, and background of the garden. To see whether a tour is offered, check the schedule.

d) Attend Special activities: The Savill Garden conducts several activities all year long, such as workshops, plant sales, and garden festivals. To get the most out of your stay, keep an eye on the event schedule.

4.4 Highclere Castle (Downton Abbey)

The nearby town of Newbury's Highclere Castle rose to popularity as the main shooting site for the hit television program "Downton Abbey." Here are some things you should know about this historical and cultural treasure:

a) Take a guided tour of the castle to see the lavish interior of Highclere Castle, which includes the State Rooms and bedrooms. Admire the ornate architecture, stunning artwork, and vintage decor that immerses you in the "Downton Abbey" setting.

b) Wander around the beautifully planted grounds that surround the castle to learn more about them. The gardens provide a peaceful escape and spectacular views of the surrounding countryside, from the placid lawns to the colorful flower beds.

c) Visit the Egyptian Exhibition: The 5th Earl of Carnarvon's discoveries in Egypt, notably the tomb of Tutankhamun, are shown at the Egyptian Exhibition at Highclere Castle. Investigate the exhibit to learn more about this interesting facet of the castle's past.

d) Attend Special Events: Throughout the year, Highclere Castle holds several events, including summer concerts, Christmas markets, and themed exhibits. Plan your visit based on the event information available on the castle's website.

4.5 Basildon Park

A beautiful park surrounds the stately Georgian home Basildon Park, which is close to Reading. What to anticipate while touring this gem of architecture is as follows:

a) Explore the Mansion: Enter Basildon Park and take in the beautifully renovated spaces that include antique furniture, fine paintings, and detailed decorations. Find out about the mansion's past residents and their families.

b) Take a leisurely walk on the grounds: The parkland that surrounds the estate is a great place to relax. Discover secret trails, take in the estate's natural splendor, and take in the tranquil environment.

c) Picnics, wildlife hikes, and children's play areas are just a few of the outdoor activities you may engage in at Basildon Park. Spend some time in nature and immerse yourself in the peace of the area.

d) Attend Events and Exhibitions: Throughout the year, the households have several events and exhibitions, including art exhibits, workshops, and themed activities. To find out what's going on during your visit, see the schedule.

These top Berkshire attractions provide a variety of experiences, from seeing old castles and gardens to taking in the thrill of horse racing. Create lasting memories during your vacation by immersing yourself in the area's rich historical, natural beauty, and cultural offers

4.6 Legoland Windsor Resort

A kid-friendly theme park called Legoland Windsor Resort may be found in Windsor, Berkshire. What you should know about this well-known attraction is as follows:

a) Theme park rides are fun: Legoland Windsor has a variety of rides and activities for visitors of all ages. There is something for everyone's taste, ranging from exhilarating roller coasters to calm rides for smaller kids.

b) Visit Miniland: This place is a must-see where millions of Lego bricks are used to reproduce well-known locations from across the globe. As the little towns come to life, awe at the minute intricacies.

c) Participate in Interactive Experiences: Legoland provides interactive activities such as building workshops where guests may let their imaginations run wild and construct their own Lego creations. Immerse yourself in the Lego universe and take part in the excitement.

d) Splash about in the Water Park: A separate Water Park is also available at Legoland, which is great for cooling down on warm summer days. Enjoy a cool aquatic journey with water slides, splash pads, and a lazy river.

4.7 Reading Abbey Ruins

The Reading Abbey Ruins are a historic location in the city. What makes it a must-see attraction is as follows:

a) Walk amid the ruins and imagine the magnificence of this significant monastic complex, Reading Abbey, which was built in 1121 by King Henry I, to learn about medieval history.

b) Visit the Abbey Gateway, which is the only whole original abbey building still standing. Learn about its historical importance while admiring its stunning architecture.

c) Enjoy Guided Tours: Take a guided tour to learn more about the history and architectural characteristics of the abbey. Interesting tales and an insight into medieval life will be shared by knowledgeable guides.

d) Attend Events and Exhibitions: The Reading Abbey Ruins often hold events and exhibitions, such as concerts, historical reenactments, and art exhibits. When you come, check the calendar for future activities.

4.8 The Living Rainforest

The Living Rainforest is a distinctive indoor tropical rainforest attraction that is located in Hampstead Norreys. Here's what to anticipate:

a) Discover Tropical Biodiversity: Enter The Living Rainforest's lush environment to find a wide variety of unusual plants, animals, and birds. Explore the high pathways and get up close to intriguing species.

b) Discover more about conservation: The Living Rainforest strives to increase public understanding of rainforest sustainability and protection. Educational exhibits and hands-on activities provide insightful information on the significance of protecting these priceless ecosystems.

c) Attend Animal Feeding Events: Attend animal feeding events to see animals being fed, including monkeys, sloths, and reptiles, while they savor their meals. Learn about their diets and habits from the staff's wealth of expertise.

d) Take a break in the on-site café, which serves a variety of beverages and snacks. Or browse the gift shop. Browse the gift store for sustainable and green trinkets including apparel, toys, and books.

4.9 Shaw House

Shaw House in Newbury is a magnificent Elizabethan house with a colorful past. Here are some reasons to go:

a) Discover Architectural Beauty: Shaw House is a beautiful example of Elizabethan architecture. Admire the ornately carved woodwork, stunning landscaping, and expansive interior areas.

b) Step inside the estate to see the exhibition rooms, which include interactive exhibits, historical objects, and furnishings from the era. Discover the amazing history of the home and the people who once called it home.

c) Take a leisurely walk around the immaculately kept grounds that surround Shaw House to enjoy them. Enjoy the calming ambiance, well-kept lawns, and colorful flower beds.

d) Attend courses & Events Shaw House conducts several courses, events, and activities all year round. This historic landmark often hosts interesting events, such as historical reenactments and artisan workshops.

4.10 Beale Park

Lower Basildon is home to the family-friendly wildlife park and gardens known as Beale Park. Here's what to anticipate:

a) Learn About Wildlife: Meerkats, monkeys, birds, and agricultural animals may all be found at Beale Park. Explore the park's expansive grounds to find diverse international wildlife.

b) Enjoy the Kids' Activities: There are several kids' activities available in the park, including a toy train ride, adventure playgrounds, and wading pools. Kids will also love visiting the gardens with a wildlife theme and feeding the ducks.

c) Relax in the Gardens: Beale Park offers lovely gardens with magnificent water features, quiet lakes, and serene picnic spaces. Enjoy the surroundings' natural splendor by taking a leisurely walk.

d) Attend Keeper Talks and displays: The park offers the opportunity to learn more about the species and their protection throughout the day by hosting educational keeper talks and animal displays.

e) These top Berkshire tourist destinations provide a wide variety of experiences, from thrilling theme parks to ethereal gardens and ancient ruins. As you come, immerse yourself in the cultural and natural attractions of Berkshire and make lifelong memories.

Chapter 5: Outdoor Activities in Berkshire

5.1 Walking and Hiking Trails

Several hiking and walking routes in Berkshire highlight the region's breathtaking natural scenery. Here are a few noteworthy choices:

a) Follow the historic Ridgeway trail as it winds 87 miles through the breathtaking North Wessex Downs Area of Outstanding Natural Beauty. Along the route, take in the expansive vistas, the rolling hills, and the historic landmarks.

b);The Thames Path: Take a stroll along the Thames Path to take in all the grandeur of the River Thames. Over 180 miles long, this route passes through Berkshire and has stunning riverside scenery and quaint villages.

c) Explore the peaceful landscape along the Kennet and Avon Canal on the Kennet and Avon Canal Path. This 87-mile trail travels beside the old canal and passes through quaint towns, locks, and verdant scenery.

d) Wander across the sizable Windsor Great Park's extensive network of walking pathways. Enjoy the park's gardens, lakes, and forests, especially the lovely Long Walk, for their tranquil beauty.

5.2 Cycling Routes

Excellent riding routes are available in Berkshire for cyclists of all skill levels. Here are a few well-liked choices:

a) The Kennet and Avon Canal Towpath: Take a flat and beautiful cycling journey along the magnificent Kennet and Avon Canal Towpath. Enjoy the tranquil canal vistas as you travel through the picturesque countryside and villages.

b) All skill levels of mountain bikers may find a network of routes at Swinley Forest, which is close to Bracknell. Experience exhilarating rides through the forest on terrain that range from easy to difficult.

c) Route from Maidenhead to Windsor Riverside: Take a leisurely bike ride from Maidenhead to Windsor Riverside along the Thames Path. This picturesque path passes by famous sites including Windsor Castle and provides stunning riverbank vistas.

d) The Greenway: Reading, Newbury, and Thatcham are just a few of the Berkshire towns connected by this authorized bicycle route. Cycling on this off-road path is risk-free and fun.

5.3 Boating and Water Sports

The canals in Berkshire provide chances for a range of boating and watersports activities. Here are a few possibilities:

a) River Thames: Several watersports are available on the River Thames, including canoeing, paddleboarding, and kayaking. Discover the peaceful parts of the river, take in the natural surroundings, and enjoy some watersports.

b) Dinton Pastures Country Park: Dinton Pastures Country Park is located close to Wokingham and has several lakes where people may go sailing, windsurfing, and fishing. Additionally, the park provides classes and equipment rentals.

c) Bray Lake Watersports is a well-liked location for sailing, stand-up paddleboarding, and windsurfing and is close to Maidenhead. To spend a day on the water, take lessons, or rent the necessary gear.

5.4 Golf Courses

Several top-notch golf courses in Berkshire welcome both experienced players and novices. Here are a few standout choices:

a) One of the best golf clubs in the UK is Sunningdale Golf Club, which has two championship courses nestled amid stunning countryside. Numerous notable golf competitions have been held there.

b) The Red Course and the Blue Course, two 18-hole courses, are available at the prestigious Berkshire Golf Club. Take advantage of the difficult fairways, beautiful surroundings, and top-notch playing conditions.

c) The Castle Royle Golf & Country Club has a championship golf course with beautiful scenery and a difficult layout. Additionally, the club has a pro shop, practice areas, and golf instruction.

5.5 Fishing Options

Anglers have great fishing options in Berkshire. Here are a few well-liked fishing locations:

a) River Thames: Fish species found in the River Thames include roach, perch, pike, and chub. The river has several areas where fishing is permitted, but you must have the appropriate permissions.

b) Theale Fisheries is a well-known fishing complex with three lakes that are stocked with a variety of fish, such as carp, tench, and bream. There are day passes and rentals for fishing gear available.

d) Braybrooke Lake: Close to Bracknell, Braybrooke Lake is a serene fishing location renowned for its specimen carp and other coarse fish. Fishing equipment may be rented, and day tickets are available.

5.6 Wildlife Sanctuary

There are several wildlife sanctuaries in Berkshire where guests may see and enjoy the area's varied flora and animals. A few places to visit are listed below:

a) The Natural Discovery Centre is a place with interactive displays, bird hides, and natural trails close to Thatcham. Discover the ponds and forests of the reserve and discover many bird species there.

b) Hosehill Lake: Hosehill Lake is a wildlife reserve close to Theale that is well-known for its abundant birds. Visit bird hides, stroll the nature paths, and keep a lookout for kingfishers, herons, and other waterfowl.

c) Wildmoor Heath: A heathland reserve with a variety of fauna, Wildmoor Heath is close to Crowthorne. Enjoy the walking paths, look for different kinds of birds, butterflies, and reptiles, and take in the surrounding area's breathtaking natural splendor.

d) Berkshire provides a broad variety of outdoor pleasures to suit every interest and skill level, whether you like hiking along gorgeous paths, cycling along attractive roads, enjoying watersports, playing golf, fishing, or watching animals. Experience the natural beauty of the area firsthand and build lifelong memories among its alluring settings.

Chapter 6: Cultural Experiences

6.1 Galleries and Museums

There are several museums and galleries in Berkshire that provide fascinating cultural experiences. Here are a few standout choices:

a) The Reading Museum is a museum with a wide variety of exhibitions, including displays of local history, artwork, and items from archaeology. Investigate the town's history to learn intriguing details about its past.

b) The University of Reading's campus is home to the Museum of English Rural Life, which honors the heritage and culture of rural England. It has a huge collection of agricultural artifacts, images, and pictures.

c) The Stanley Spencer Gallery, which is situated near Cookham, is devoted to the creations of famous British artist Sir Stanley Spencer. Admire his unique paintings and learn more about his creative philosophy.

d) West Berkshire Museum: The West Berkshire Museum is located in Newbury and has exhibits on regional history, archaeology, and natural history. Enjoy interactive exhibits ideal for all ages while learning about the rich past of the area.

6.2 Theaters and the Performing Arts

Theaters and other performance spaces in Berkshire feature a diverse variety of plays, musicals, and other acts. Here are a few noteworthy locations:

a) The Hexagon in Reading is a well-known facility that hosts a wide variety of live activities, including theater, music concerts, comedy shows, and dance performances.

b) The Corn Exchange in Newbury is a center for the arts and hosts a variety of live activities, including comedic performances, musical performances, and theatrical shows.

c) The Wilde Theatre in Bracknell presents a diverse range of theatrical events, including classic plays and modern productions, as well as music and dance acts. The Wilde Theatre is a component of South Hill Park Arts Centre.

d) A variety of cultural events are held at the Norden Farm Centre for the Arts in Maidenhead, including theatrical shows, comedic performances, live music events, and movie screenings. The facility also provides seminars and workshops for people of all ages.

6.3 Festivals and Music
Every year, Berkshire holds several music festivals and events that appeal to a range of

musical inclinations. Here are some noteworthy points:

a) Reading Festival: One of the most well-known music events in the UK is the Reading Festival, which takes place in August. Rock, indie, and alternative bands are among the many performers on the bill, drawing music fans from all across the nation.

b) Henley Festival: This yearly event in Henley-on-Thames features a variety of performances in the fields of music, comedy, art, and cuisine. Enjoy concerts by famous artists with the River Thames as a background.

c) The September Windsor Festival honors classical music by offering performances by prominent performers and ensembles. The event also includes discussions, seminars, and displays of visual arts.

d) Eat Reading Live is a food and music event that takes place in Reading and highlights regional cuisine and live musical acts. Enjoy the flavorful cuisine and the lively ambiance.

6.4 Food and Drinking Experiences

The culinary scene in Berkshire provides a wide variety of dining and drinking options. Here are a few suggestions:

a) Fine dining and gastropubs: Berkshire is home to a variety of fine dining and gastro pubs that serve a range of cuisines, including classic British meals and tastes from across the world. Enjoy delicious meals that are made using ingredients that are locally sourced.

b) Afternoon Tea: Indulge in a classic British custom by taking afternoon tea in one of Berkshire's lovely hotels or tea shops. Enjoy tasty teas, scones with jam and clotted cream, and dainty sandwiches.

c) Farmers' Markets: Visit farmers' markets like the Reading Farmers' Market and the Newbury Artisan Market to sample the regional cuisine. Directly from the farmers, sample fresh food, handcrafted goods, and regional specialties.

d) Tours of local breweries and wineries are a great way to learn about Berkshire's rich brewing and winemaking history.

Discover the manufacturing methods, taste the drinks, and get knowledge of the area's brewing and viticulture customs.

6.5 Local Markets and Stores

For those looking for one-of-a-kind gifts, regional goods, and retail therapy, Berkshire has a wide selection of markets and shopping locations. Here are a few noteworthy choices:

a) The Reading Market is a bustling marketplace with a variety of booths offering goods including fresh vegetables, crafts, apparel, and more. It is situated in the center of Reading. Examine the diverse selection of items and take in the vibrant ambiance.

b) Windsor Royal Retail is a picturesque retail district housed in historical structures and is located close to Windsor Castle. Explore a range of boutiques, artisanal shops, and businesses that sell apparel, presents, and mementos.

c) The Oracle Shopping Centre is a contemporary shopping center with a variety of high-street brands, fashion retailers, dining establishments, and entertainment venues. It is situated in Reading.

d) Visit the antique stores and vintage boutiques in places like Cookham and Hungerford. Find one-of-a-kind rarities, vintage treasures, and antique furniture.

e) Farm stores: Buy locally produced food and handcrafted goods at one of the many farm stores located around Berkshire. Fresh produce, including fruits, vegetables, meats, and cheeses, is available at these stores, all of it coming directly from local farmers.

f) Immerse yourself in Berkshire's diverse cultural attractions, which range from museums and art galleries to energetic music festivals, dining possibilities, and specialty shops. As you come, embrace the county's unique cultural scene and make lifelong memories.

Chapter 7: Hidden Gems and Insider's Tips

7.1 Off-the-Beaten-Path Attractions

Berkshire is more than simply its well-known sights; it also has undiscovered treasures that provide uncommon and off-the-beaten-path experiences. Here are a few lesser-known sights that are worthwhile visiting:

a) Visit the Roman city of Calleva Atrebatum, which is close to Silchester, and its amphitheater. Discover the historic city walls and the amphitheater, which sometimes holds events and concerts.

b) The majestic Elizabethan house Mapledurham House, which is located on the banks of the River Thames, is open for guided visits. Nearby is the Watermill. Explore its beautiful gardens and historical buildings, and pay a visit to the adjacent, one of the nation's oldest running watermills.

c) Explore the ancient hill figure etched into the chalk hills at Uffington White Horse and Dragon Hill. Visit the neighboring mound known as Dragon Hill for a climb and take in the expansive views of the surrounding landscape.

d) Discover the lovely Greys Court, a Tudor-style manor home close to Henley-on-Thames. Explore the estate's stunning gardens, historic forests, and secret nooks to get a full sense of its tranquility and history.

e) Visit the Maharaja's Well in Stoke Poges, the city's undiscovered treasure. The well was constructed in the 19th century as a gift from an Indian maharaja to provide fresh water to the neighborhood. Discover the rich history while admiring the beautiful design.

7.2 Local Festivals and Events

Numerous community gatherings and festivals are held throughout Berkshire, and they provide a window into the rich culture and customs of the area. Here are a few suggestions:

a) Henley Regatta: Attend the renowned Henley Regatta, an annual rowing competition held in Henley-on-Thames. Take in the vibrant atmosphere of this major sports event while watching spectacular races and taking in riverbank entertainment.

b) Attend the Newbury Show, an agricultural exhibition exhibiting the finest of Berkshire's rural life. Enjoy animal presentations, local product displays, handmade crafts, and family-friendly activities.

c) Easthampstead Park Open Air Cinema: In the summer, Bracknell's Easthampstead Park plays home to outdoor movie showings. Bring a blanket for a picnic, settle down for a movie beneath the stars, and take in the scenery.

d) Join the fun at the Wokingham May Fayre, a yearly celebration that takes place on the May Day holiday. Discover live performances, fairground attractions, regional crafts, and mouthwatering food vendors.

7.3 Recommended Cafes and Restaurants

With a variety of eateries to suit every taste, Berkshire has a vibrant culinary scene. Here are some businesses we suggest you visit:

a) Visit the famed Michelin-starred restaurant The Fat Duck in Bray for a gourmet journey. Discover cutting-edge, artistically created delicacies that push the frontiers of cuisine.

b) Discover a delicious dining experience at L'Ortolan in Shinfield, a Michelin-starred restaurant close to Reading. Enjoy a wide selection of wines with delectable French cuisine in a chic and exclusive atmosphere.

c) In a lovely riverfront setting, Coppa Club in Sonning-on-Thames provides a laid-back ambiance and varied cuisine that includes wood-fired pizzas, shared platters, and energizing drinks.

d) Enjoy outstanding food at the beautiful riverside restaurant The French Horn in Sonning-on-Thames. It provides a memorable dining experience with its stunning vistas and sophisticated British delicacies on the menu.

d) Visit Tuttis in Reading, a lively café renowned for its delectable vegetarian and vegan fare. Enjoy a variety of nutritious selections, such as salads, smoothie bowls, and inventive plant-based cuisine.

e) Discover The Woodspeen in Newbury, a restaurant and cooking school housed in a former farm structure. It serves a seasonal cuisine with locally produced products that are influenced by British and Mediterranean influences.

f) Be sure to explore Berkshire beyond the well-known sights and take advantage of the local culture and hidden treasures that give the area its unique character. These insider ideas can help you discover the lesser-known gems and make priceless memories while you are there, from historical places and cultural events to gastronomic pleasures.

7.4 Insider's Shopping Spots

There are various undiscovered shops in Berkshire where you may get one-of-a-kind items and regional goods. Here are some advice from the inside:

a) Nettlebed Antique and Collectors Market is a paradise for antique enthusiasts and is situated close to Henley-on-Thames. Discover a variety of antique objects, including furniture, jewelry, pottery, and artwork, as you peruse the booths.

b) Visit the Yattendon hamlet Shop, which is located in the charming hamlet of Yattendon. Including handmade cheeses, baked pastries, fresh fruits and veggies, and other locally produced food, this charming shop provides a lovely range.

c) An undiscovered treasure for foodies is The Cobbs Farm Shop and Kitchen, which is located in Hungerford. The farm shop's shelves are stocked with regional specialties, while the on-site restaurant serves up freshly cooked meals.

d) Investigate The Emporium at The Wellington Arms in Baughurst. It is a bar and restaurant. This distinctive store offers a hand-picked assortment of gifts, home goods, and handmade goods that are obtained from regional manufacturers and small companies.

e) Thames Hospice Warehouse: If you're looking to support a good cause, the Windsor location of the Thames Hospice Warehouse has a treasure trove of gently used products, including apparel, furniture, books, and household items. Discover hidden jewels while helping a worthy cause.

7.5 Day Trips from Berkshire

The central position of Berkshire gives it the ideal starting point for visiting neighboring landmarks and activities. Here are a few suggested day trips:

a) Visit the ancient city of Oxford for the day; it's just a short drive from Berkshire. Visit its museums and art galleries, see its renowned university buildings, and wander the quaint alleys dotted with boutiques and cafés.

b) Visit Bath, a city renowned for its Georgian architecture and Roman baths. Visit the magnificent Bath Abbey, go on a guided tour of the Roman Baths, and stroll through the charming alleyways lined with small shops and eateries.

c) Discover the ancient city of Winchester, known for its cathedral and allure of the Middle Ages. Explore the historic alleyways of Winchester, visit the cathedral, and take advantage of the city's thriving arts scene and independent retailers.

d) Salisbury: Take a tour of this charming city and stop at the Salisbury Cathedral, which houses the fabled Magna Carta. Explore the ancient Salisbury Market, wander around the city's historic streets, and take in the friendly ambiance.

e) Take a beautiful drive through the picture-perfect countryside of the Cotswolds. Visit historical places like Blenheim Palace, explore quaint villages with thatched cottages, and take in the tranquility and natural beauty of the region.

These day tours provide you the chance to explore the adjacent regions' fascinating histories, beautiful buildings, and scenic landscapes, expanding your discovery beyond Berkshire and helping you to make long-lasting memories of your vacation.

Chapter 8: Helpful Practical Travel Information

8.1 Website and Emergency Contacts

Here are crucial phone numbers and a useful website in case of an emergency while you're in Berkshire:

a) Emergency Services: Dial 999 for ambulance, police, or fire services if you need urgent help in a life-threatening emergency.

b) Non-Emergency Police: Dial 101 to report a non-emergency situation or for non-urgent police help.

c) NHS Non-Emergency Medical support: Call the NHS 111 service if you need non-emergency medical advice or support.

d) Visit the Berkshire County Council's official website at www.berkshire.gov.uk for information and services related to the area, including travel and tourism.

8.2 Health and Safety Tips

Take into account the following advice to guarantee a secure and healthy trip to Berkshire:

a) Get thorough travel insurance before your journey to cover any unforeseen medical costs, trip cancellations, or lost possessions.

b) Medical Care: If you need medical assistance, Berkshire is home to several hospitals and clinics. Visit a walk-in clinic or ask a local pharmacist for help if you need medical care for anything that isn't an emergency.

c) Take reasonable safety measures and be cautious, just as you would in any other place. Watch out for your possessions, especially in busy places, and use caution while traveling by public transit.

d) Outdoor Safety: Make sure you're well-prepared if you want to partake in outdoor activities like cycling or hiking. To prevent mishaps, dress adequately, carry enough water, and abide by safety rules.

8.3 Banking and Currency

The British Pound Sterling (£) is used as money across the United Kingdom, including Berkshire. Here are some suggestions about banking and money:

a) Cash machines, usually referred to as ATMs, are readily accessible throughout Berkshire. You may withdraw money in GBP using major debit and credit cards that are accepted there.

To be sure your card will function overseas, let your bank know before you go.

b) Currency Exchange: In bigger towns and cities, banks, post offices, and currency exchange offices provide currency exchange services. Before converting money, compare exchange rates and costs.

c) Credit and debit cards are generally accepted at most businesses, including hotels, eateries, and retail stores. For little transactions or locations that may not take cards, it's best to have some cash on hand.

8.4 Internet and Communication

In Berkshire, staying connected and using the internet are both quite simple tasks. The following are some crucial considerations:

a) Mobile Networks: In the UK, EE, O2, Vodafone, and Three are some of the top mobile network providers. If required, check with your service provider to make sure your cell phone is configured for international roaming, or think about buying a local SIM card.

b) Wi-Fi: In Berkshire, the majority of hotels, cafés, restaurants, and public places have free Wi-Fi connectivity. Additionally, libraries and internet cafés provide access to the internet.

c) Dialing internationally: To call abroad, enter the international access code (often + or 00), then the country code and the number. Without the country code, dial the local number to reach a local number in Berkshire.

8.5 Useful Expressions

Although Berkshire's official language is English, understanding a few basic phrases might be useful when you are there. These words and phrases are helpful:

Hello

Goodbye

Please

Thank you

Excuse me

Do you speak English?

I need help

Where is...?

How much does it cost?

Can I have the bill, please?

Keep in mind that most people in Berkshire are pleasant and courteous and that English is their primary language. Even with simple words and phrases, trying to communicate in their language is always appreciated.

Chapter 9: Additional Information and Resources

9.1 Family Vacations Tips

There are many family-friendly activities and attractions in Berkshire that can be enjoyed by people of all ages. Here are some pointers for planning a special family trip to Berkshire:

a) Theme parks: For a day full of exhilarating rides and family entertainment, check out the neighboring Thorpe Park or the Legoland Windsor Resort.

b) Wildlife Encounters: Visit wildlife parks and sanctuaries where kids may see and learn about various species and habitats, such as Beale Park and The Living Rainforest.

c) Historical Sites: Introduce kids to history by taking them to places like Reading Abbey

Ruins, Basildon Park, or Windsor Castle, where they may learn about the area's rich legacy.

d) Outdoor Adventures: Take part in outdoor activities including biking, hiking, and boating in beautiful places like Dinton Pastures Country Park, Windsor Great Park, and the Kennet and Avon Canal.

e) Check local event calendars for family-friendly festivals, fairs, and other special events taking place while you are visiting Berkshire.

9.2 Romantic Adventures Guide

Couples looking for romantic settings may find them in Berkshire. Following are some pointers for a romantic getaway in Berkshire:

a) Romantic Strolls: Enjoy a stroll along the River Thames, a romantic lunch on the grounds of Cliveden House, or a tour of Shaw House's gardens.

b) Fine Dining: Treat your significant other to a special supper at one of Berkshire's finest establishments, including The Fat Duck in Bray or L'Ortolan in Shinfield, all of which provide cozy ambiance and delectable cuisine.

c) River Cruises: Take a romantic boat ride down the River Thames where you may take in the beautiful scenery, relish a delectable meal, or drink champagne while taking in the scene.

d) Spa retreats: Indulge in a romantic spa getaway for two at one of Berkshire's opulent spas, such as Coworth Park or Nirvana Spa, where you may unwind and revitalize one another.

e) Find a vantage point to see a magnificent sunset, such as from a hilltop in the North Wessex Downs or from Cookham's Thames Path.

9.3 Travel Tips for Solo Travelers

For lone travelers, Berkshire provides a pleasant and secure atmosphere. To maximize your solo experience, consider the following advice:

a) Join Guided Tours: To connect with visitors and locals who have similar interests, think about participating in guided tours or other events. It's a fantastic opportunity to discover the area and meet new people.

b) Cultural Experiences: By visiting museums, going to live performances, or discovering undiscovered attractions suggested in our travel guide, you may fully immerse yourself in the local culture.

c) Choose lodgings that promote social contact among visitors, such as hostels or guesthouses, to stay in. This offers chances to interact with and learn from other travelers.

d) Talk to locals: Engage them in conversation in cafés, markets, or cultural events. They may provide suggestions, insider knowledge, and perceptions of the region's best-kept secrets.

e) Safety Advice: As a lone traveler, pay attention to your security. Inform someone of your vacation intentions, safeguard essential papers, and use caution while venturing out at night in unknown regions.

9.4 Suggested Itineraries

You may organize your journey in Berkshire using the following two recommended itineraries:

History and Culture Tour

- Day 1: Take a tour of Windsor Castle and meander around Windsor Great Park's lovely gardens.

- Day 2: Explore Basildon Park and savor the heritage of this magnificent residence. Explore Reading in the afternoon, then stop at the Reading Museum.

- Day 3: Take a stroll along the Kennet and Avon Canal Towpath and see the Reading Abbey Ruins.

- Day 4: Explore the lovely hamlet of Newbury, including a trip to the West

Berkshire Museum, and pay a visit to
Highclere Castle (Downton Abbey).

- Day 5: Spend the day at
Henley-on-Thames, taking in the town's
ancient architecture and taking a boat
trip down the Thames.

Nature and Outdoor Activities
- Day 1: To fully experience tropical
biodiversity, start the day with a trip to
The Living Rainforest. Investigate Beale
Park's lovely lakes and gardens in the late
afternoon.

- Day 2: Spend the day biking or trekking
the Ridgeway National Trail and taking
in the breathtaking views of the North
Wessex Downs.

- Day 3: Go mountain biking in Swinley Forest or have a stroll in Windsor Great Park.

- Day 4: Take a boat excursion or go fishing to see the natural splendor of the Kennet and Avon Canal. Visit Dinton Pastures Country Park for leisurely walks or water sports.

- Day 5: Take a day excursion from Berkshire to the picturesque towns and farmland of the Cotswolds to experience the beauty and peace of the area.

You are welcome to modify these itineraries to suit your interests, time constraints, and desired rate of exploration.

Chapter 10: Conclusion

The allure of Berkshire lies in its unique combination of history, culture, scenic beauty, and thrilling adventures. Every traveler may find something to enjoy in Berkshire, whether they are interested in history, nature, gastronomy, or culture.

There are several options to make unforgettable experiences and fully immerse yourself in the beauty of the area, from touring famous sights like Windsor Castle and Ascot Racecourse to finding hidden treasures like Mapledurham House and Nettlebed Antique Market.

You now have a thorough overview of Berkshire's attractions, useful information, and insider recommendations to make the most of your trip thanks to our succinct and thorough travel guide. You'll discover suggestions catered to your hobbies and travel preferences whether you're organizing a family vacation, a romantic getaway, or a solitary journey.

Recommendations

To acquire lodging, tickets, and meal reservations, we strongly advise that you take the time to plan your schedule and make bookings in advance, particularly during busy travel times. It's also a good idea to check for any new COVID-19-related travel limitations, regional regulations, or particular requirements before your trip.

Last but not least, when you visit Berkshire, remember to embrace the spirit of exploration and adventure. Engage the community, sample the cuisine, and take the time to savor the region's natural beauty and historical importance. Your trip to Berkshire will undoubtedly be full of treasured memories, insider discoveries, and unique experiences if you have this travel guide at your side.

Made in the USA
Monee, IL
24 September 2023